Slut For Grief

Poems of Loss, Lust, and Rebirth

Sara Reed

BookLeaf Publishing

India | USA | UK

Made with ❤ on the BookLeaf Publishing Platform
www.bookleafpub.in
www.bookleafpub.com

Dedication

To mom and dad

Preface

This collection of fiercely raw poems explores the tangled emotions of loss and longing, grief and desire, capturing the messy beauty of rebirth and resilience. *Slut for Grief* expertly dances between devastating heartache and the sheer audacity of hope—because sometimes, the most profound truths are found during the darkest of times. Are you ready to feel?

Acknowledgements

Thank you Ed and Cathy for your undying love. Thank you Kate, Jen, Katie, Nima, Kelly, Jason, Biggie, the Scheffeys, the Reeds, and the Snitgers. Thank you sex toys and Lexapro and pickles and online shopping for pre-owned luxury handbags. I somehow emerged from the dark, wounded, yet alive. Thank you, thank you, thank you.

1. the first week

I talk to strangers about you
I hide this wound away from those who know me
Those who knew you
They might smudge it and make me forget you
Or worse, make me remember a little bit too much

So I talk to strangers about you
I tell them how much you not only loved me
but that you really fucking liked me
And they say how rare that is
And I say I worry no one will ever love me like that
again

And maybe they won't.

Maybe that's the love you only get from the woman who
grew you in her womb and nourished you with her body
and heart and soul.

I talk to strangers about you
I tell them how proud I am of you
How we had adventures
How no one understands
I tell them about your kindness and your heart and how

you gave some of that to me
I think they see it in me too

2. lost on me

It's not lost on me
that you sent that ocean breeze
through Harrisburg
the day I needed it

3. creature of grief

I have become a creature of grief
An animal that hides in the darkest spots
In the latest hours
I have become a sponge
Thick, deep holes
Wanting to be filled by everyone and everything
I tend to my wounds
Late at night
When the world sleeps
When the thick air chokes
When my body refuses sleep
Sometimes I am not sure what I am grieving
I just know my belly is hallow with missing
I am haunted by lost wishes and hopes
That have nowhere to go
I purge them in the darkness
Force them from my eyes, falling down my cheeks
I choke on them and wonder
When will they be done?

4. i see you when i look in the mirror

I see you when I look in the mirror
The way the corners of my mouth
Turn down when no one is looking
When I'm not trying to look pretty
My birthday is next week
My belly is empty and hollow
I took you to the ocean
I mixed you into the sand
Ground you between my fingers
Bone and shells
You disappeared into the foaming waves
Skin and salt
I can't look in the mirror without seeing your face
The corners of your mouth turning down
When no one is looking

5. to be of use

To be of warm skin and liquid
Of pouty red and the rise and fall of breath
Of soft trembling fingers
Eyes that look down with nerves
But most with need
To be of the smoothest slip of the finger
Past the pout and onto the slick tongue
The smell of wet grass
Of your need
Of vanilla in my hair
To be of thick, roundness that parts
Only at the exact right moment
Like clouds parting and warm, liquid sunshine
But only for you
To be of soft mounds, of hard peaks
The breath that escapes the lips
Of a slow letting go
Of a handing over
I pass my body to you
To be of use

6. dancing

Under gray skies
Plates of French fries
Tears in my eyes
but still learning to live without you

I dream of days, sun on my face,
Eyes wide shut, honey warm rays
I'm figuring it all out now
How to live without you

7. it smells like a library

It smells like a library
Like a bookstore
Like home
Like incense in a church
Like memories that never got made
Deep and musky and grazing the tip of my heart
It smells like cool wind kicking up dead flowers
Like an apple left to rot on the street
It smells like my green camo jacket, thick and heavy
To hid under and beneath
Like the words my lips can't quite form
It smells like hope and tears and freedoms sitting on a
table just waiting to be snatched
It smells like you

8. gun or cock

I am sick and tired of waiting for a man to love me half
as much as I can
And to understand how it feels to walk alone at night
Keys between my fingers, scared for my life
With your poking and your prodding and your please
send a pic
Searching for your mommy while driven by your dick
And then expect me to open my door for you
Expect me to open my legs for you too
As if you'll understand the first thing about what to do
Spoiler alert: you don't make me come
You're up and out the door, on to the next one
Women are the only mammals to mate with their killers
And you wonder why we're so obsessed with murderers
and thrillers
Get down on your knees he says with glee
Is it a gun or a cock? How can you tell us we're free?

9. i miss home

I miss home
Not home the place
Home the feeling
It's the warm linoleum floor in the summer
It's falling asleep to the sound of baseball
It's a feeling tucked deep in my belly
Made of longing and sorrow and safety
It's not often I find
Or feel
Home
These days

10. untitled 54

I will load the boxes into my car
I will pile my art into the trunk
With nothing to protect it
I will close the doors
I will hope for the best

My heart will bleed as I turn right
It leaves drops
And streaks
In the streets
In the Jersey sun

When I reach the state line
It will be dry

I'm sorry I was too hard to love

When I reach the sunshine
It will be dry

I'm sorry I was so hard to love

11. a vessel

They ask how it feels
Fingers carving my insides
Filled with something new

12. Serenity II

Your clothes are still in my drawers
like you're haunting my home
Like you'll walk through the door
with a sweaty kiss
Hi everyone
I miss you like I miss home
Deep in my belly
Like I miss Christmas
And summer sunshine
First her, now you
I put your earring in my ear
It was the last part of you inside me
Like those days that felt like magic
I threw our puzzle in the trash
We always thought we'd finish it
Please come home

13. CW

I turned myself inside out for you
Exposed

14. call from the porch

That day on the porch when you called me
I told you it didn't have to hurt like this
Hidden bottles where I couldn't reach
The girl you invited in
Sinking stomach
Shaking hands
Did you know it would ruin everything?

15. yard sale day

Creaky old wooden bedframe
We talked about living on a farm
A few kids
Rings on our fingers
You cried in bed
Did you know then that you would walk away?

16. men

When I let them in
They eat my insides like starving wolves
Nails and sharpened teeth
Scraping, pulling, emptying
Replacing with their body
All in the name of wanting to be liked
She looked so good when she was last seen

17. his name is ari

I told you no monkey business
And then you entered my space
Like an animal eyeing his prey
To fill and push and make a dent
To use my holes as if they belonged to you
I told you no monkey business

18. a poem for the girls who are hard to love

Why is it that the smallest men
Are the ones who claim
We are hard to love?
Is it because we are made of magic?
We are messy like water overflowing out of an already
overfilled glass
We are waterfalls of words and tears and loud thoughts
and quiet moments
We are not hard to love, we are hard to contain

19. operating theater for the broken hearted

Deep in the inky sky
They came to my bedside
Tiny scalpel shimmers in the light
It's time to make things right
Again

They work for hours
Digging and pulling up
The weeds like flowers
Removing every sweet and salty
Memory of you

Like that day at beach
When the sand hurt our feet
And I played you Taylor Swift
It never was a lift
To love you

I've asked for this
For a brain that could exist
Without every sweet and sour
Memory of you

20. he who shall not be named

When we do bad things
In secret, lust takes over
Bright light through the blinds

I'm wearing that dress
The one with the sunflowers
Before my life changed

When things were simple
When words could cure the hunger
Not so simple now

21. what comes after

Sharp winter air stings my nostrils
Guess what?
I'm breathing again

www.ingramcontent.com/pod-product-compliance
Lightning Source LLC
Chambersburg PA
CBHW070731160726
48003CB00006BA/2444